Lee Evans arranges

easy JAZZ STANDARDS

T0042562

Contents

Second Edition

HAL•LEONARD®
CORPORATION
77 W. BLUEMOUND RD. P.O. BOX 13819
MILWAUKEE, WISCONSIN 53213

ANGEL EYES

Words by EARL BRENT
Music by MATT DENNIS
Arranged by LEE EVANS

Moderately slow (♩ = 88)

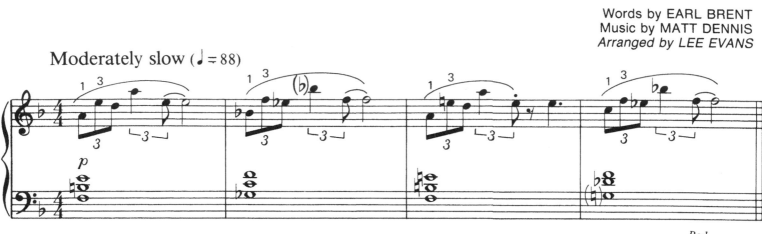

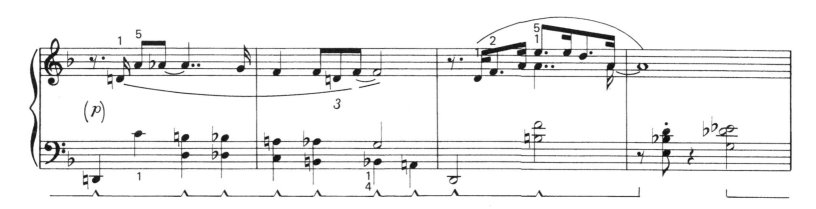

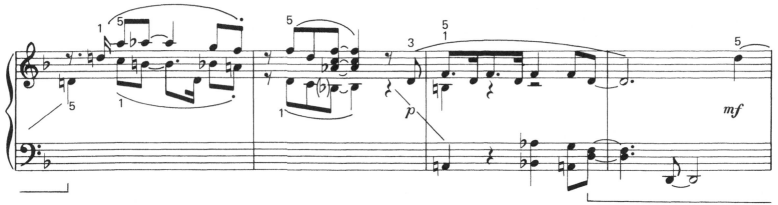

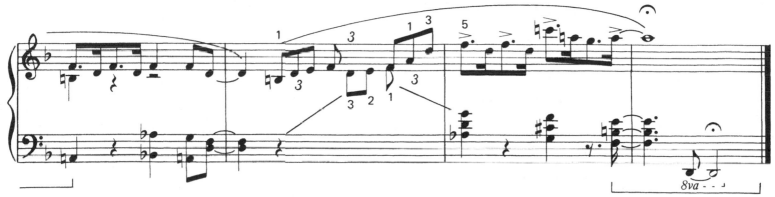

HERE'S THAT RAINY DAY

Words and Music by
JOHNNY BURKE and JAMES VAN HEUSEN
Arranged by LEE EVANS

Ballad tempo; rubato (♩ = 58)

LULLABY OF THE LEAVES

Words by JOE YOUNG
Music by BERNICE PETKERE
Arranged by LEE EVANS

With a lilt (♩ = 126)

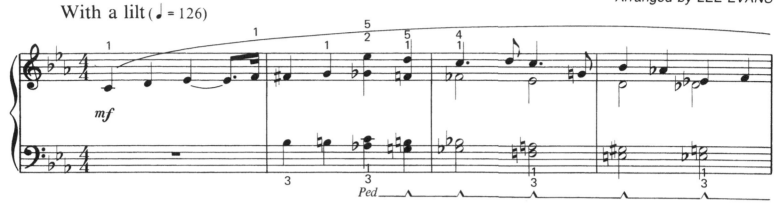

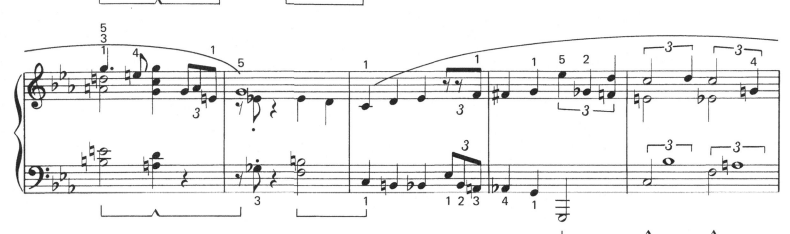

8

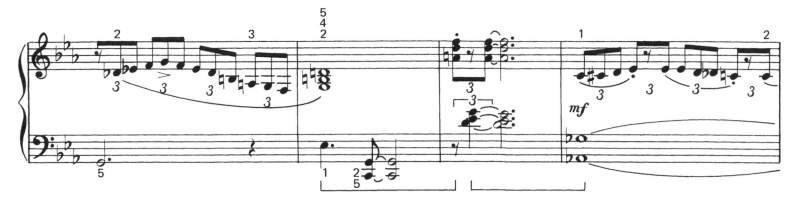

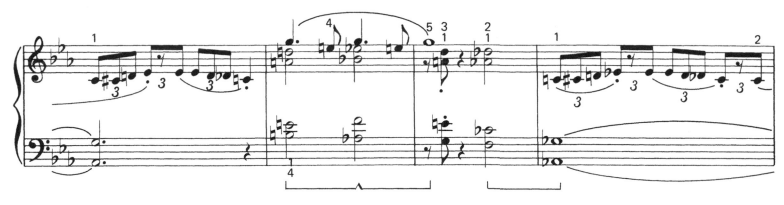

NO MOON AT ALL

Words and Music by
REED EVANS and DAVE MANN
Arranged by LEE EVANS

Swing feel (♩ = 152)

(No pedal)

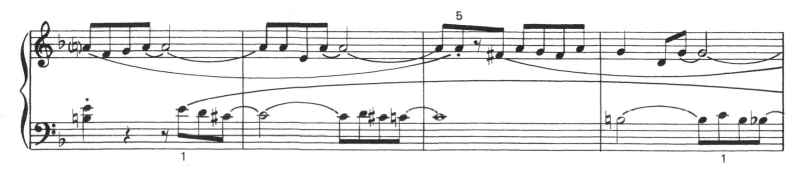

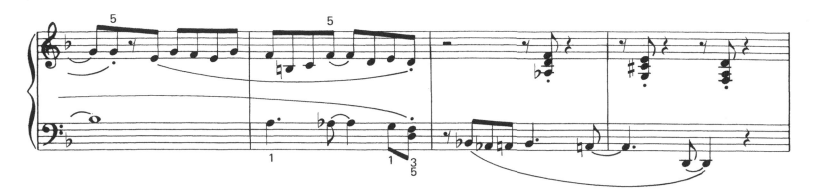

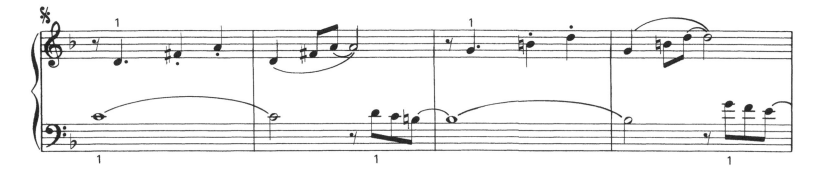

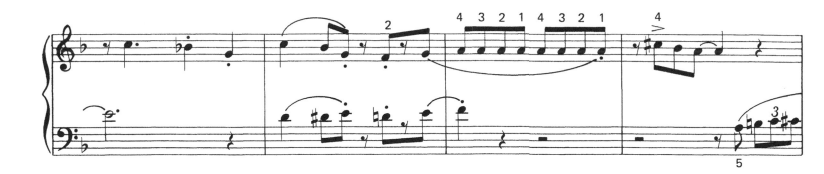

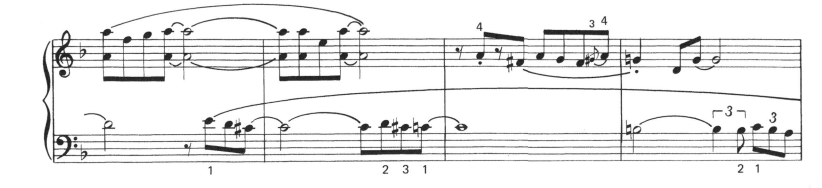

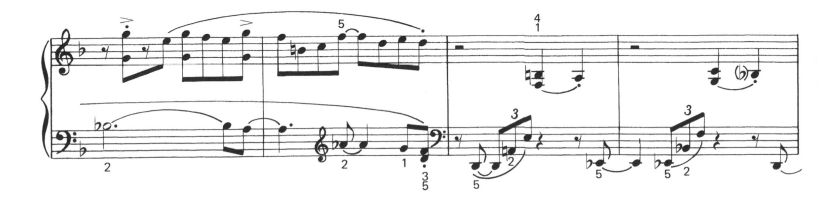

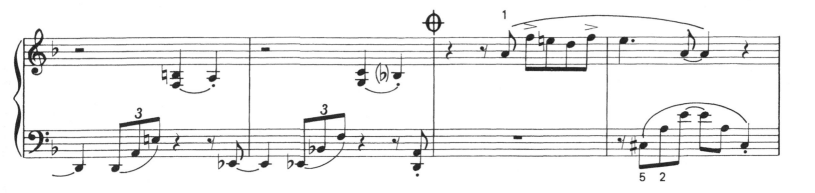

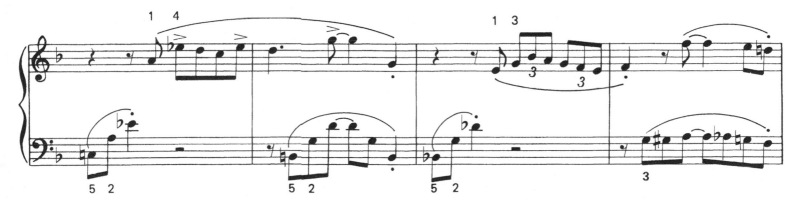

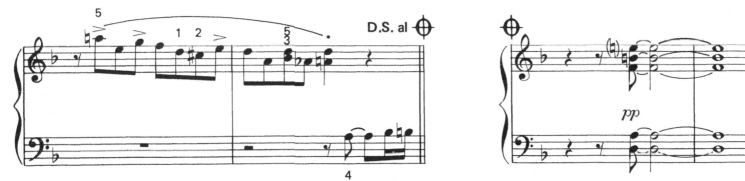

THERE'S A SMALL HOTEL

(From "ON YOUR TOES")

Words by LORENZ HART
Music by RICHARD RODGERS
Arranged by LEE EVANS

Rubato; ballad tempo (circa ♩ = 58)

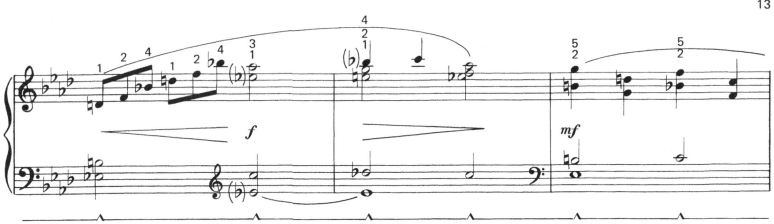

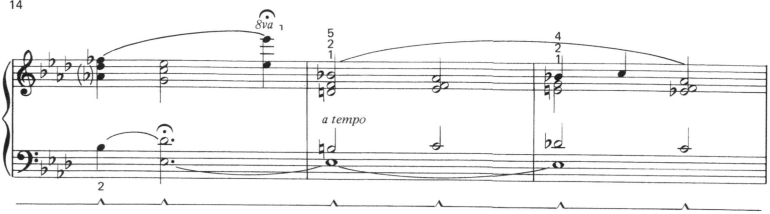

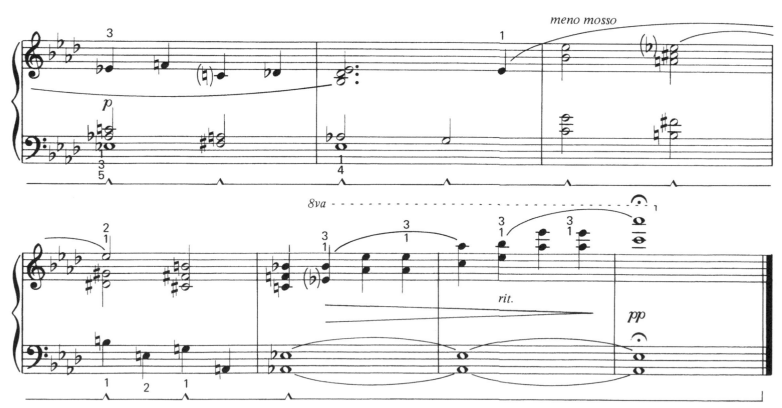

NICE WORK IF YOU CAN GET IT

Words by IRA GERSHWIN
Music by GEORGE GERSHWIN
Arranged by LEE EVANS

Medium bounce (♩ = 132)

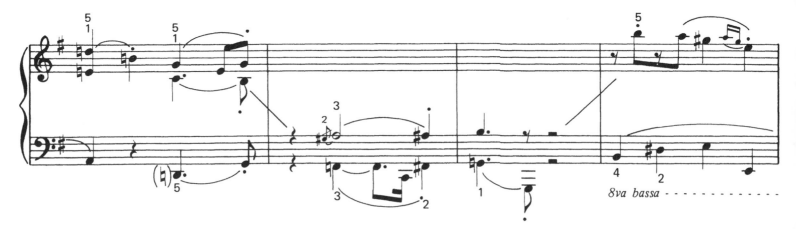

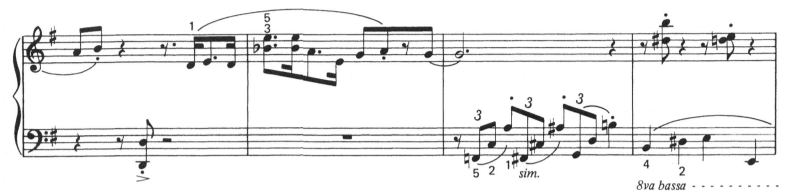

D.S. al ⊕

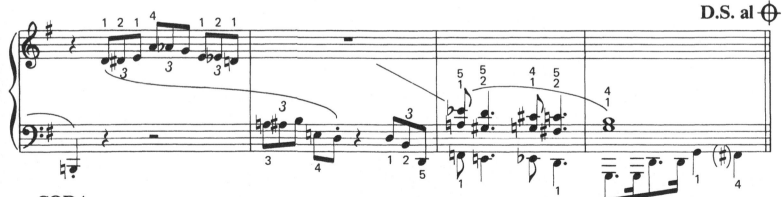

CODA

ROBBIN'S NEST

By SIR CHARLES THOMPSON
and "ILLINOIS" JACQUET
Arranged by LEE EVANS

Moderate bounce (♩ = 132)

(No pedal throughout)

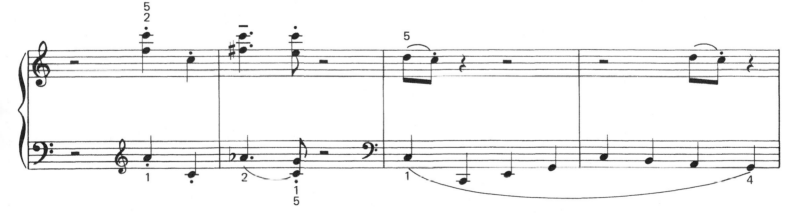

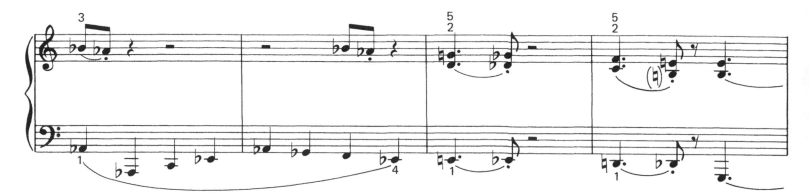

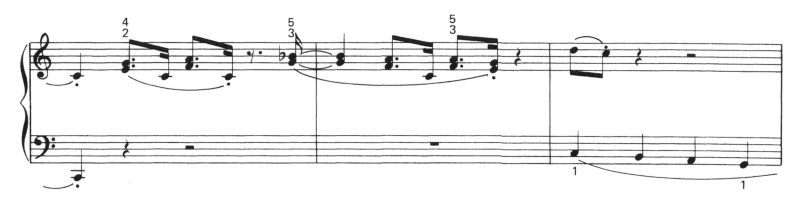

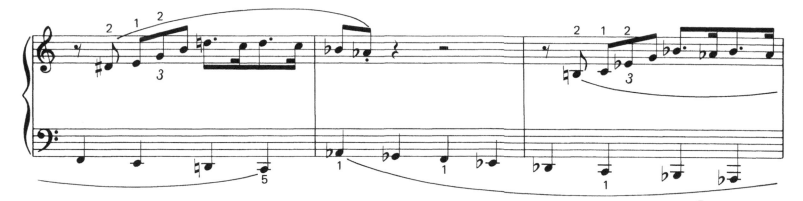

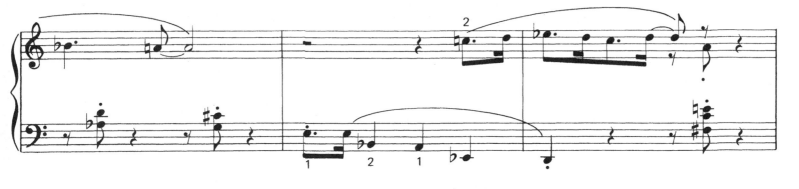

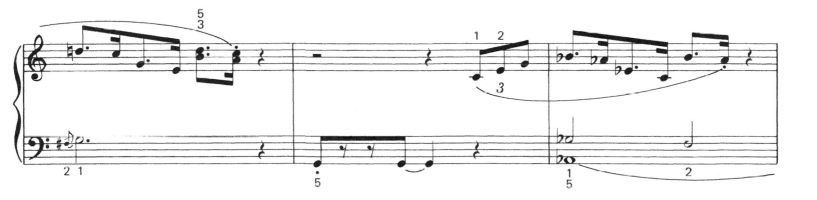

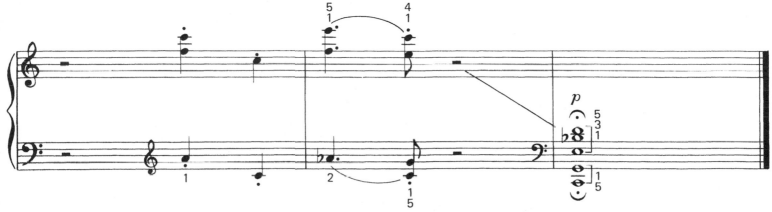

COME RAIN OR COME SHINE

Words by JOHNNY MERCER
Music by HAROLD ARLEN
Arranged by LEE EVANS

Slow Blues Feel (♩ = 92)

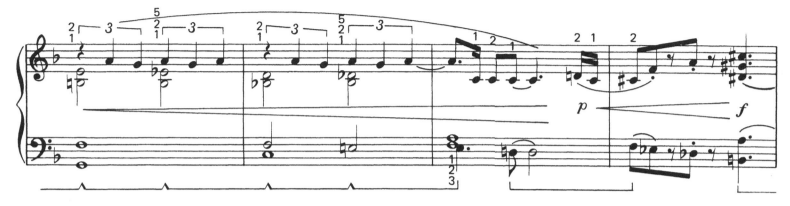

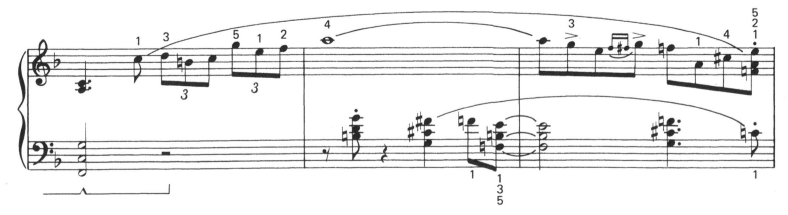

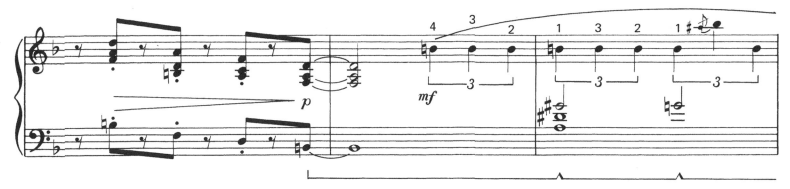

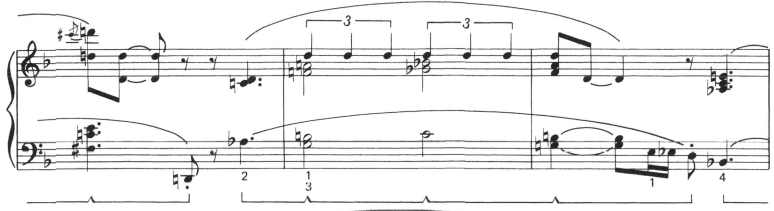

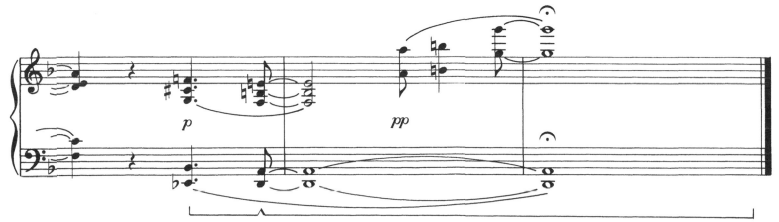

A NIGHTINGALE SANG
IN BERKELEY SQUARE

Lyric by ERIC MASCHWITZ
Music by MANNING SHERWIN
Arranged by LEE EVANS

Moderately; Rubato (circa ♩ = 92)

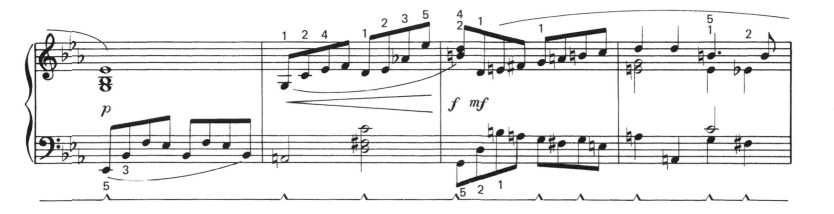

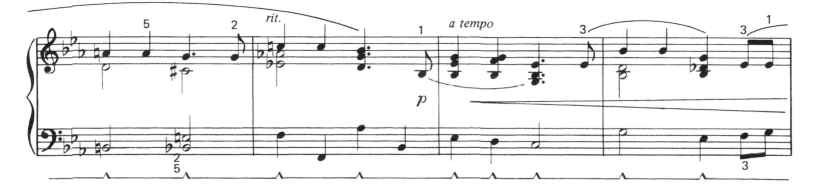

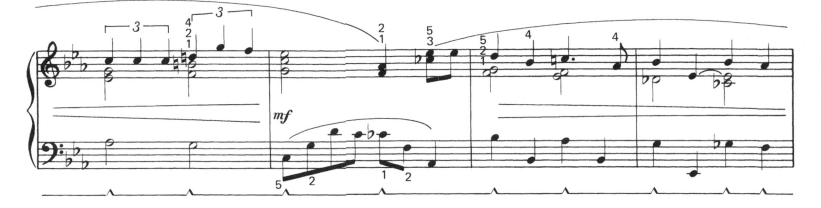

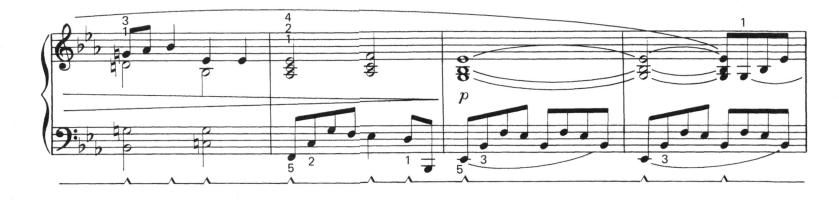

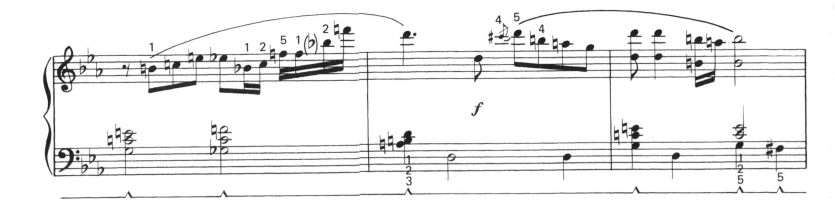

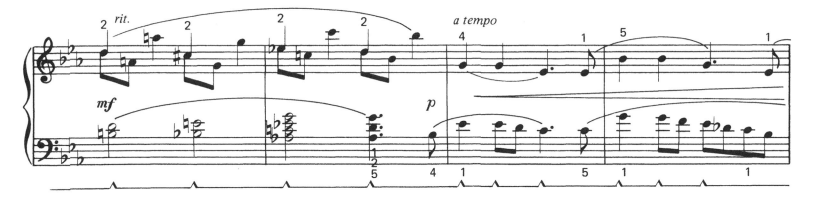

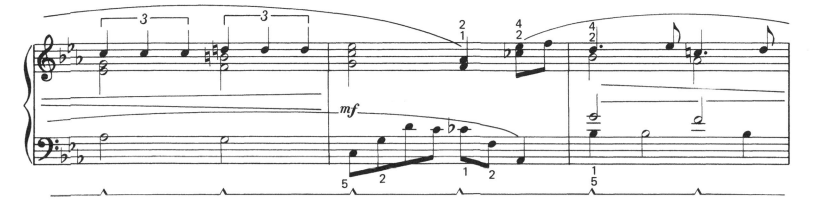

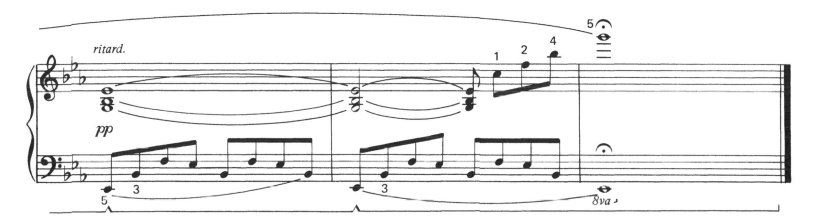

EAST OF THE SUN
(And West Of The Moon)

Words and Music by BROOKS BOWMAN
Arranged by LEE EVANS

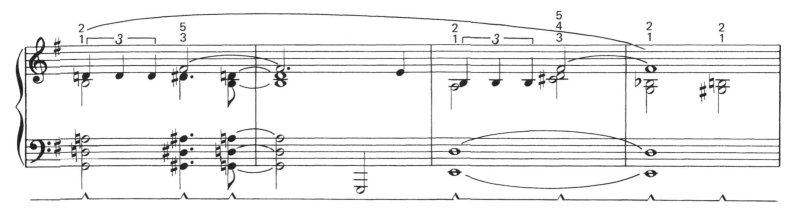

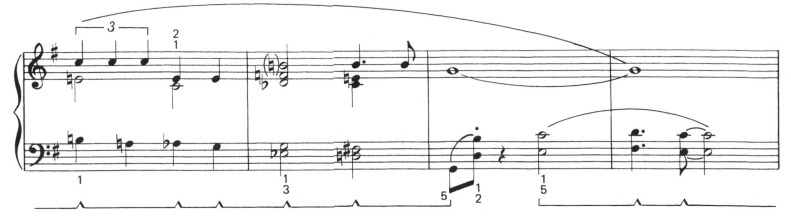

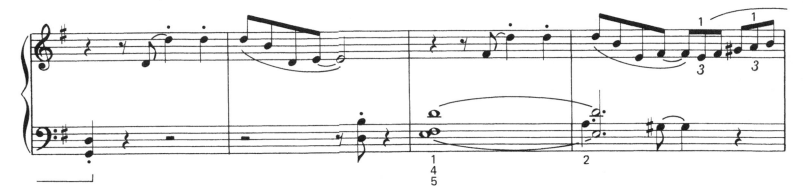

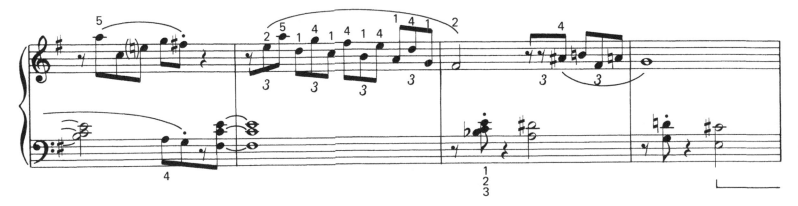

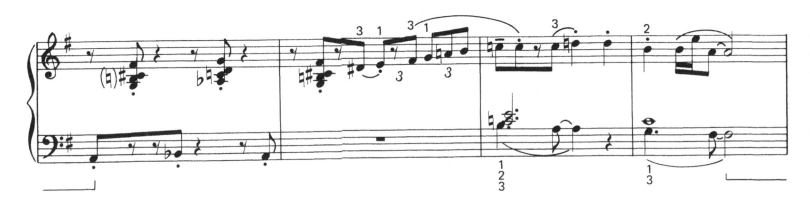

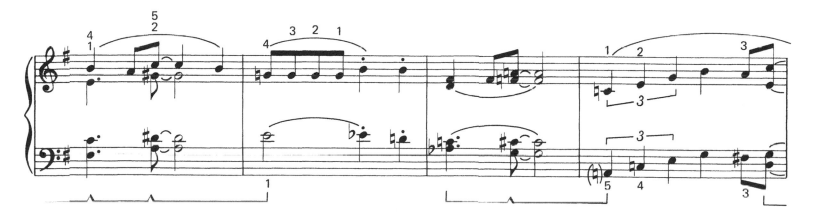

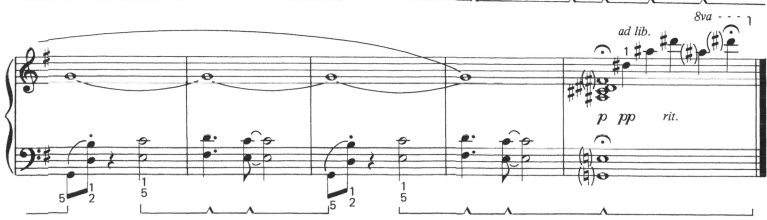

'DEED I DO

Words and Music by
WALTER HIRSCH and FRED ROSE
Arranged by LEE EVANS

Moderate bounce tempo (♩ = 116)

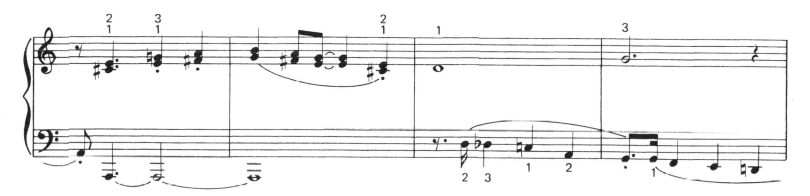

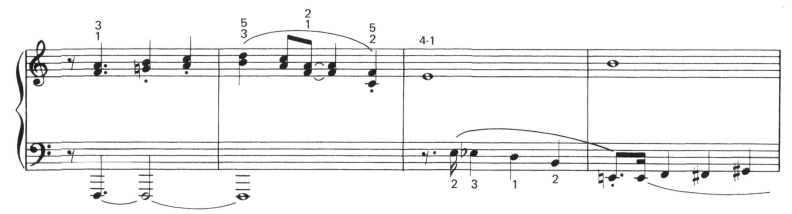

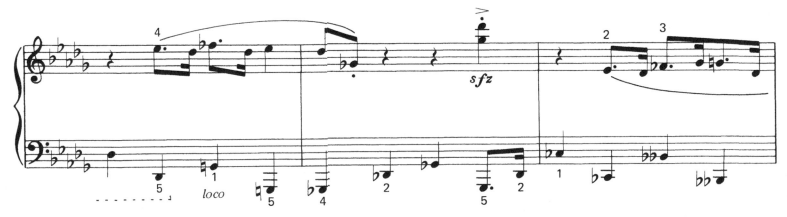

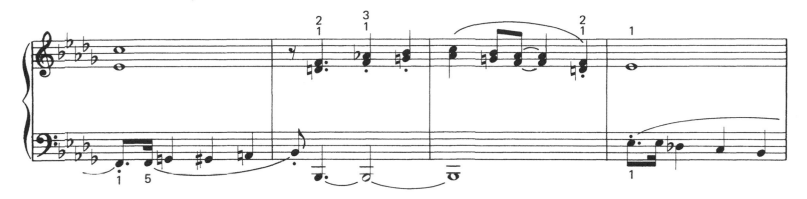

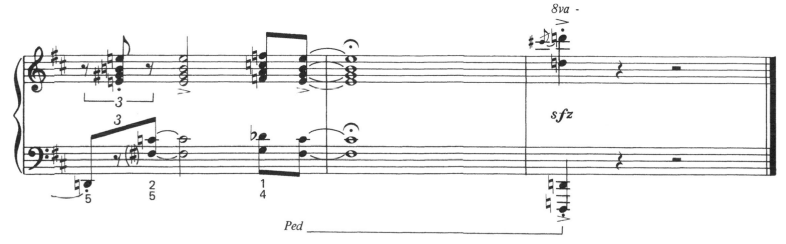

I COULD WRITE A BOOK

(From "PAL JOEY")

Words by LORENZ HART
Music by RICHARD RODGERS
Arranged by LEE EVANS

Molto Rubato; Expressively

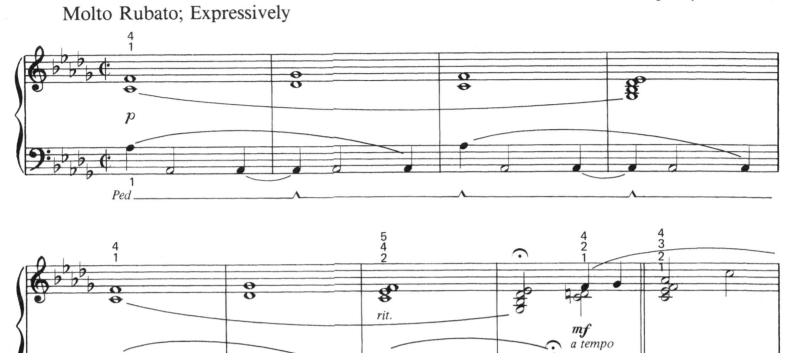

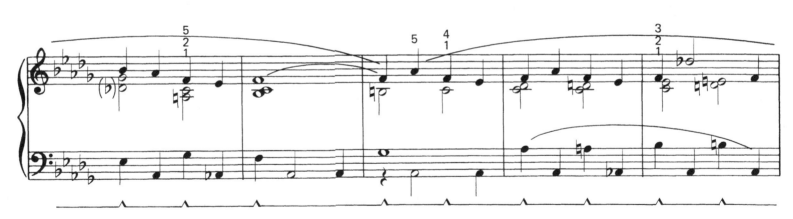

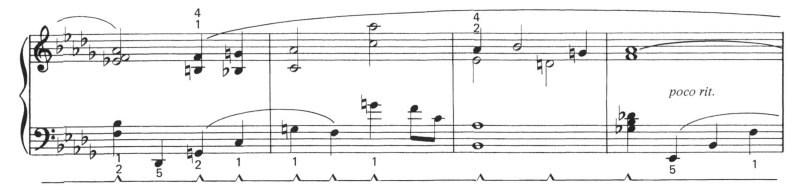

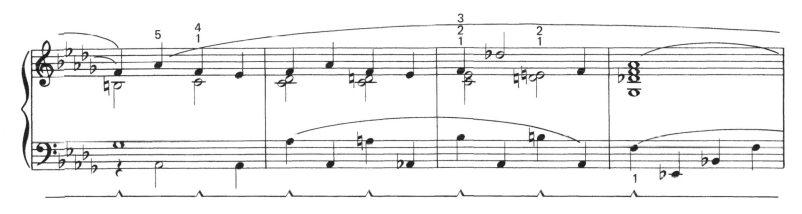

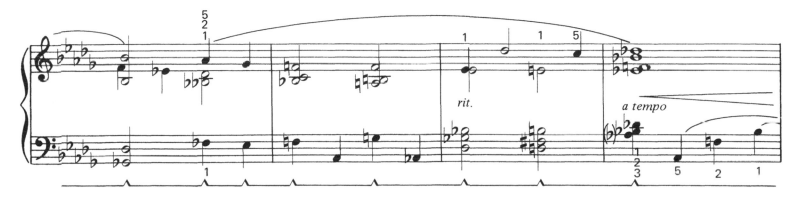

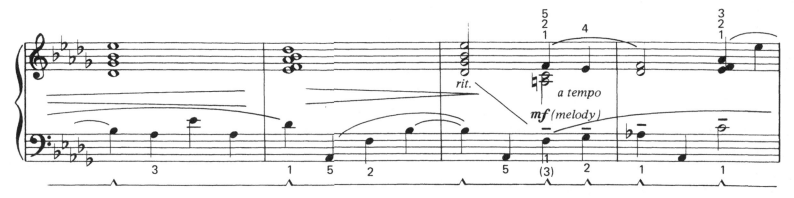

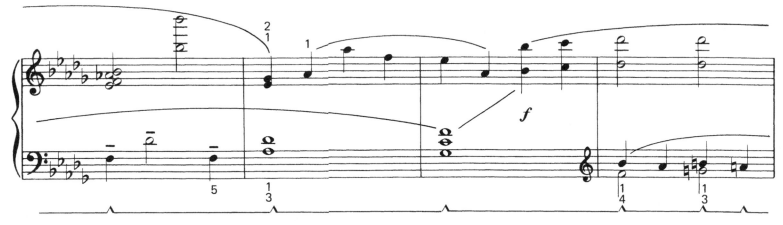

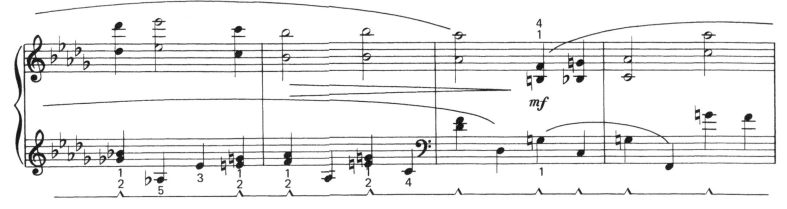

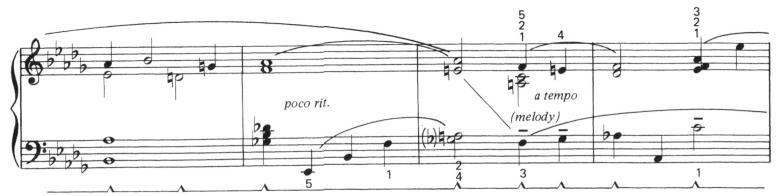

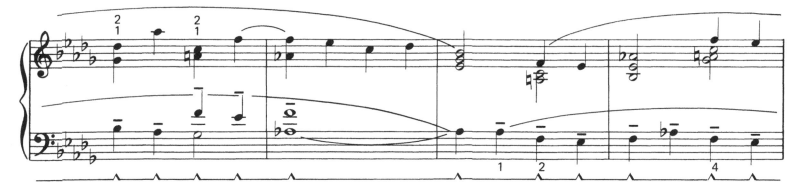

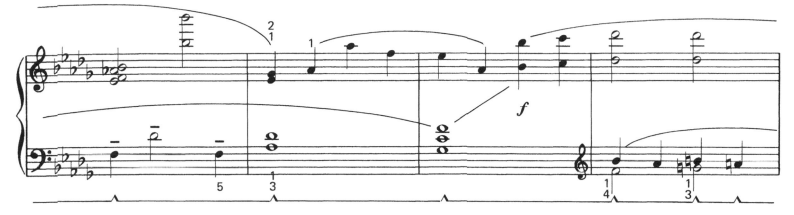

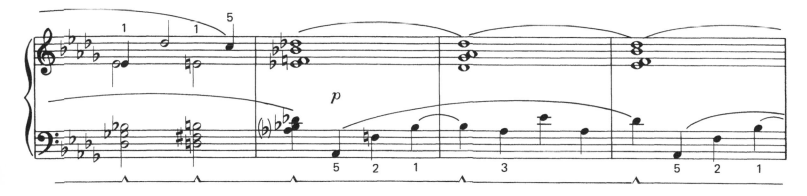

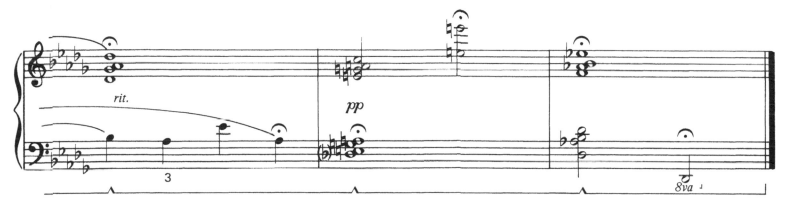

YOU TURNED THE TABLES ON ME

Words by SIDNEY D. MITCHELL
Music by LOUIS ALTER
Arranged by LEE EVANS

Easy bounce (♩ = 112)

(No pedal throughout)

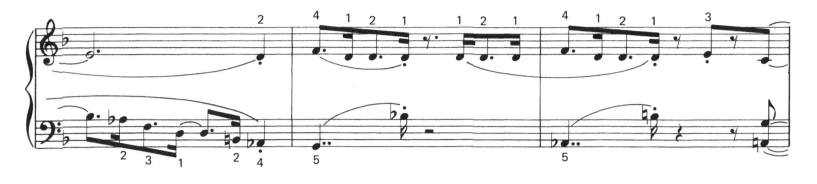

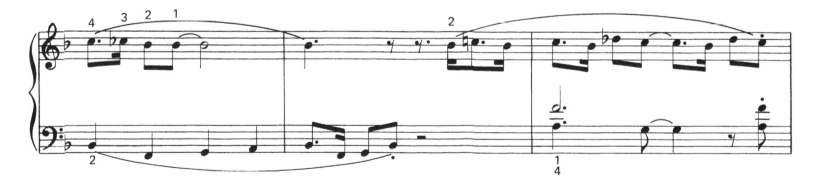

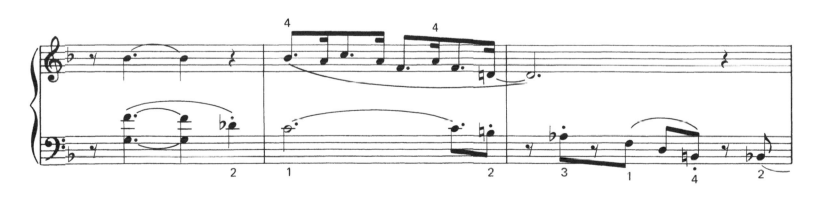

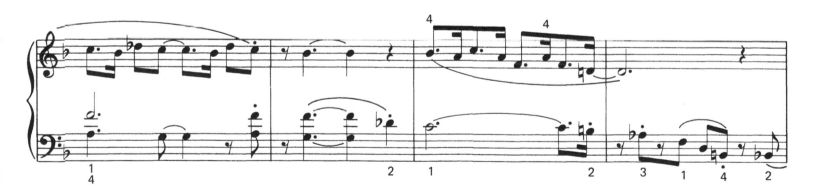

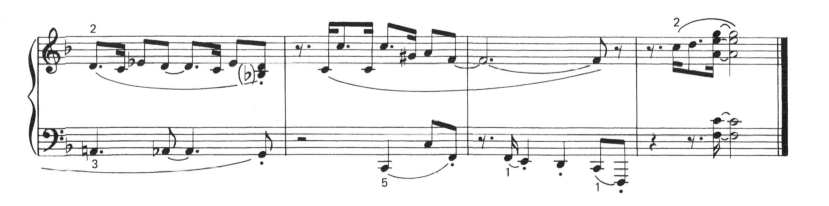

BERNIE'S TUNE

By BERNIE MILLER
Arranged by LEE EVANS

Fast (♩=120)

(No pedal)

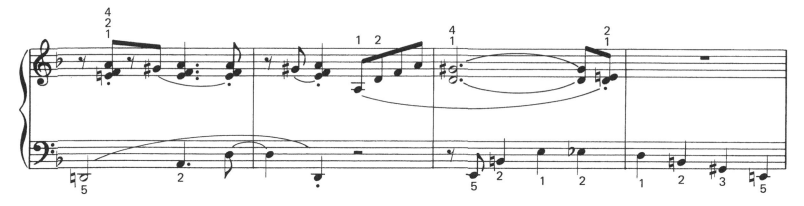

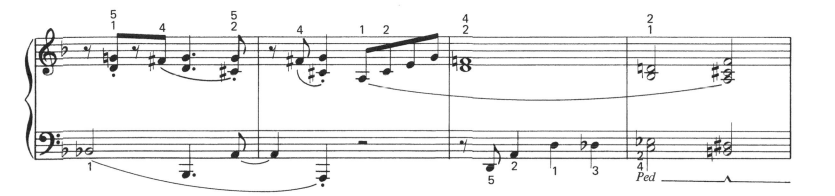

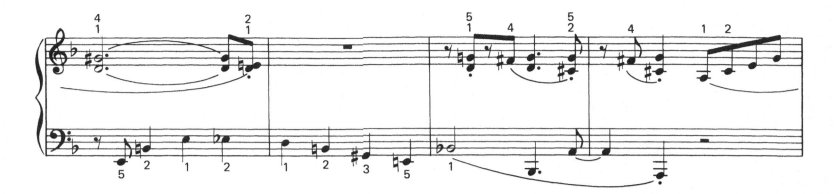